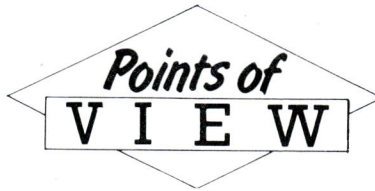

Points of VIEW

·D·I·V·O·R·C·E·

Ann Mitchell

Wayland

Points of View

Abortion
Advertising
Alcohol
Animal Rights
Apartheid
Capital Punishment
Censorship
Divorce

Drugs
Medical Ethics
Northern Ireland
Nuclear Weapons
Racism
Sex and Sexuality
Smoking
Terrorism

Front cover: *Some marriages simply do not work, but in such circumstances, what is the best solution?*

Excerpts from *Second Chances* by Sandra Blakeslee and Judith S. Wallerstein. Copyright © 1989 by Sandra Blakeslee and Judith S. Wallerstein. Reprinted by permission of Houghton Mifflin Company.

Editor: William Wharfe
Designer: David Armitage

First published in 1990 by
Wayland (Publishers) Limited
61 Western Road, Hove
East Sussex BN3 1JD, England

British Library Cataloguing in Publication Data
Mitchell, Ann, 1922 –
    Divorce. – (Points of view).
    1. England. Married persons. Separation & divorce – Manuals
    I. Title   II. Series
    306.8'9'0942

ISBN 1-85210-800-2

Phototypeset by Direct Image Photosetting Ltd, Hove, East Sussex, England.
Printed in Italy by G. Canale & C.S.p.A., Turin
Bound in France by A.G.M.

Contents

1 Introduction

Divorce is the legal ending of a marriage between a husband and a wife. It means the dissolution of a marriage by judgement of a court or by accepted custom. Marriage can also be ended by separation, either informally without any public or legal action, or judicially (that is, by means of a legal document). After separation, the partners are still legally married to each other. Separation without divorce happens all over the world, but is most usual in countries that do not allow divorce, such as Ireland. As the social historian, Ferdinand Mount, put it in 1983, 'Past centuries might not permit divorce in the modern sense, but poor men simply divorced themselves by running away.'

Why does anyone need divorce?

> If the world were ideal, there would be no necessity for any laws which would put an end to the tie [of marriage] but . . . some marriages become complete failures and life together becomes either morally or physically impossible. (Lord Gorell, chairman of the Royal Commission on Marriage and Divorce, 1912).

Henry VIII, King of England (1509–1547). His divorce from his first wife, Catherine of Aragon, involved the separation of the Christian Church in England from the control of the Pope. Henry eventually married a further five times, divorcing another wife and beheading two.

A Hindu wedding in India. Such marriages are usually arranged by the parents, so the bride and groom are sometimes strangers to one another. This may lead to problems later on.

Katharine Whitehorn, journalist, put two views in the *Observer* newspaper on 27 March 1988:

> A country where there is no divorce is going to have some desperately unhappy people trapped in rotten marriages; equally where divorce devours one marriage in two, as in some parts of America, the human damage will be staggering.

A tale is told in a nineteenth century Indian legend of what happened when divorce was abolished:

> The following inscription is written in large characters over the principal gate of the city of Agra, in Hindustan: 'In the first year of the reign of King Julief, two thousand married couples were separated, by the magistrates, with their own consent. The emperor was so indignant, on learning these particulars, that he abolished the privilege of divorce. In the course of the following year, the number of marriages in Agra was less than before by three thousand; the number of adulteries was greater by seven thousand; three hundred women were burned alive for poisoning their husbands; seventy-five men were burned for the murder of their wives; and the quantity of furniture broken and destroyed, in the interior of private families, amounted to the value of three millions of rupees. The emperor re-established the privilege of divorce.'
> (*Niles' Register*, 1825.)

Some reasons for wanting to end a marriage:
- To escape from an unhappy relationship.
- To marry someone else.
- Wife has not produced a son (especially in China).
- One partner cannot forgive the other's behaviour.
- Money difficulties.
- Excessive drinking.

Some factors that can increase the divorce rate:
- More liberal divorce laws.
- Cheaper divorce.
- Higher expectations of marriage.
- Greater equality of men and women.
- Financial aid to one-parent families.
- Longer life expectancy.
- Reduction in stigma.
- War.

Many Churches, including the early Christian Churches, believed that marriage could not be ended except by death. In many European countries, until the middle of the nineteenth century, only the Churches had the power to dissolve a marriage if it could be proved not to have been valid in the first place.

Nowadays religions have different ideas about marriage breakdown. Roman Catholics and Hindus believe that marriage lasts until the death of one partner. The Catholic Church can sometimes annul (dissolve) a marriage if there is proof that, for instance, one partner did not understand the marriage vows, or refused to consummate the marriage. The Roman Catholic and

This Roman Catholic wedding is not a private ceremony, but is publicly acknowledged by friends and relations.

DIVORCE No 26

World's most-wed man says: Young women will not stay in the home

Glynn Wolfe: "She wouldn't swep the floors!"

THE WORLD'S most married man is at it again.

Glynn "Scotty" Wolfe is seeking divorce from wife No. 26 and is on the lookout for Bride No. 27.

Filed

The 76-year-old Baptist minister conceded that marriage has not worked for him yet.

"But I'm not giving up," he announced from Blythe, California, where

By SUN REPORTER

he has filed for his un-contested 26th.

The latest marital casualty, he says, was the result of a generation gap. The old-timer complained that his 38-year-old wife wasn't home most of the time.

"These young women don't want to stay home and wash clothes and do the ironing and sweep the floor," he fumed.

Wolfe tied the knot with Christina Sue Camacho Wolfe in Las Vegas last January.

Now the never-say-die

wedder says he's looking for a wife who can do wonders in the courtroom rather than the kitchen.

The city of Blythe sued Wolfe last year to close the hotel he has owned for nearly 13 years and Wolfe now wants to sue the city for "kicking me out of my house without due process."

Famous

He would he says, put the next Mrs Wolfe on the case, " . . . give her half of a million dollars, make her famous, have some fun and let her go when she's through."

Greek or Russian Orthodox Churches do not recognize divorces granted in civil courts. In Greece and the USSR religiously devout couples must seek permission from the Church in order to divorce properly, independently of civil divorces granted by government authorities. By contrast, the Qur'an tells Muslims that it is better to divorce than to live in an unhappy marriage.

In many Western countries, the legal authorities have recognized the need for divorce laws. In 1943 Lord Simon, the Lord Chancellor of Great Britain, said:

> The interest of the community at large is to be judged by maintaining a true balance between respect for the binding sanctity of marriage and the social considerations which make it contrary to public policy to insist on the maintenance of a union which has utterly broken down.

The objectives of a good divorce law were defined by the (English) Law Commission in 1966:

> (i) to buttress, rather than to undermine, the stability of marriage; and (ii) when, regrettably, a marriage has irretrievably broken down, to enable the empty legal shell to be destroyed with the maximum fairness, and the minimum bitterness, distress and humiliation. (*Reform of the Grounds of Divorce: the Field of Choice:* Cmnd 3123, para 15.)

During this century there has been a steady increase in divorce in practically every country. In this book we will be asking why this is so and looking at different people's views on divorce.

Some people who opposed the relaxation of divorce laws foresaw the end of all long-term marriages. In fact, that did not happen, although some people do seem incapable of staying married for long!

---

1 Why do some people think an increase in the divorce rate is a bad thing?
2 Pick one or two of the reasons for increase in the divorce rate, and explain why they lead to more divorces.
3 Which is preferable, separation or divorce? Why?

Divorce around the world

The highest divorce rate in the world is in the USA. Australia, Britain and New Zealand follow close behind, in that order. One in three of present-day marriages in England and Wales are likely to end in divorce before their thirtieth anniversary. In parts of the USA the rate is as high as one in two.

Divorce has been known for many centuries. The Bible tells us:

> When a man hath taken a wife, and married her, and it comes to pass that she find no favour in his eyes, because he hath found some uncleanness in her: then let him write her a bill of divorcement and give it in her hand, and send her out of his house. (Deuteronomy, 24, i.)

However, Jesus is reported to have said: 'What God hath joined together, let not man put asunder,' (Mark, 10, ix.). These words are used today in many Christian marriage services, and are sometimes quoted by people who believe marriage to be indissoluble.

A divorce court in England in 1870. By this time divorce was well-established in English law, but if this woman wanted to divorce her husband, she had to prove cruelty or desertion by him, as well as adultery.

Up to the 1850s, in Europe, a divorce would only be granted by Christian Churches where people were able to show that the marriage was invalid; for instance, if it was never consummated. Then divorce began to be obtainable in Protestant countries. Gradually, civil courts were able to grant divorces on proof of 'a marital offence' by one partner against the other. Usually this meant adultery, with or without desertion or, later, cruelty. Some countries allowed divorce for other offences.

Divorce was introduced into English law in 1857. Previously those who wished to be divorced had had to secure a private Act of Parliament for the purpose, which was very difficult and enormously expensive, and resulted in about two divorces a year. After 1857, a husband could obtain a divorce on account of his wife's adultery; but a divorcing wife had to prove, in addition to adultery, desertion or cruelty by her husband.

Early divorce laws in the USA, Australia, Canada and New Zealand were largely based on those in England. Later, they diverged. For instance, in 1920, divorce was allowed in New Zealand after three years' separation, and in two Australian states after five years' separation, where both husband and wife agreed. Divorce was still rare in industrialized countries before the twentieth century. It was usually available only to the rich.

In Scotland, financial help could be given from the 'poor's roll' and, since the Protestant Reformation of 1560, divorce had been equally available to husbands and to wives, on grounds of adultery or desertion. Between 1836 and 1841, the Court of Session in Scotland 'pronounced 95 sentences of divorce . . . almost all of the humbler classes . . .'

In 1912, two opposite views of divorce were expressed to the British Royal Commission on Marriage and Divorce (paras 16,925 and 16,928):

> There is no good purpose to be observed by keeping people tied together for ever during their lives without the possibility of remarriage, if they are never going to live together again. (Mr J. A. Barratt, member of the US Supreme Court Bar).

> We object to divorce in itself . . . We think that the national character is quite as much benefited and raised by the patient endurance of hardships as by loosening the responsibilities of marriage. (Representative of the Mothers' Union of the Church of England.)

Factors that can lead to marriage breakdown:

- Young age at marriage.
- Pregnant before marriage.
- Poverty.
- Previous divorce (i.e. second marriage).
- Short acquaintance before marriage.
- Sexual problems.
- Disillusionment.
- Violence.
- Mixed race or religion.
- Unemployment or stressful employment.

The number of divorces is highest after marriages lasting:

Japan and Egypt	less than one year
USA, Austria and East Germany	2 years
England, Netherlands and Sweden	3 years
Australia, Denmark and Scotland	4 years
Canada and West Germany	5 years
Belgium and France	6 years
New Zealand	8 years

Divorces per 1,000 existing marriages in 1985:	
USA	21.5
Britain	13.2
Denmark	12.6
Netherlands	9.9
West Germany	8.6
France	8.1
Belgium	7.3
Japan	4.0
Portugal	3.7
Italy	1.1

Divorce is now available through civil courts in most countries of the Western world. But countries that are predominantly Roman Catholic have been reluctant to introduce divorce. Italy did so in 1971 and Spain in 1985. Divorce is still difficult to obtain in Italy, requiring five years' separation if uncontested, and seven years if contested.

Ireland is now the only Western country to allow no divorce. In an Irish referendum in 1986, a majority voted against the introduction of divorce; but there are many unhappy marriages in that country as Nuala Fennell, a junior government minister, said in 1986:

> Thousands are doomed to live lonely celibate lives or alternatively join the ranks of irregular relationships within which they are discriminated against under our social welfare and tax codes, forego legal and succession rights and have their children labelled illegitimate. (Anthony Clare, *Lovelaw,* 1986.)

Furthermore:

> In societies where divorce is difficult to obtain, there is a tendency toward dishonest annulment, fabrication of legally accepted offences, migratory divorce and legal separations. (Price and McKenry, American family specialists, *Divorce,* 1988.)

> In the nineteenth and early twentieth centuries, the divorce had to be wangled by fictitious adulteries in Brighton hotels. (Ferdinand Mount, *The Subversive Family,* 1983.)

A wedding photo of 1920. The couple probably had a long courtship and engagement, while they saved up to get married. They would have been expected to spend the rest of their lives together.

Even where divorce is readily available, 'When people are trying to get divorced, honesty is not their top priority', as a Scottish judge put it in 1984. In other words, people had to commit adultery or perjury to get a divorce.

People might find that marriage does not come up to their hopes and expectations, and so they split up:

> You get married and you're in love, and you think it'll be just like staying at home. Every young girl wants to get married. If someone asks you, you say yes. (Divorced woman, 1981, Mitchell[1].)

> I really knew it wouldn't work even before we were married, but the wedding was all arranged and I just went on with it. I suppose I thought things might change. (Divorced woman, quoted in Ailsa Burns, *Breaking Up*, 1980.)

> I wasn't really in love with my husband, but I didn't have the courage to say no to marriage. (Divorced woman, *Breaking Up*.)

There was a big increase in divorces after the Second World War. Further increases came (and have continued) following changes in laws which have made divorce more easily available.

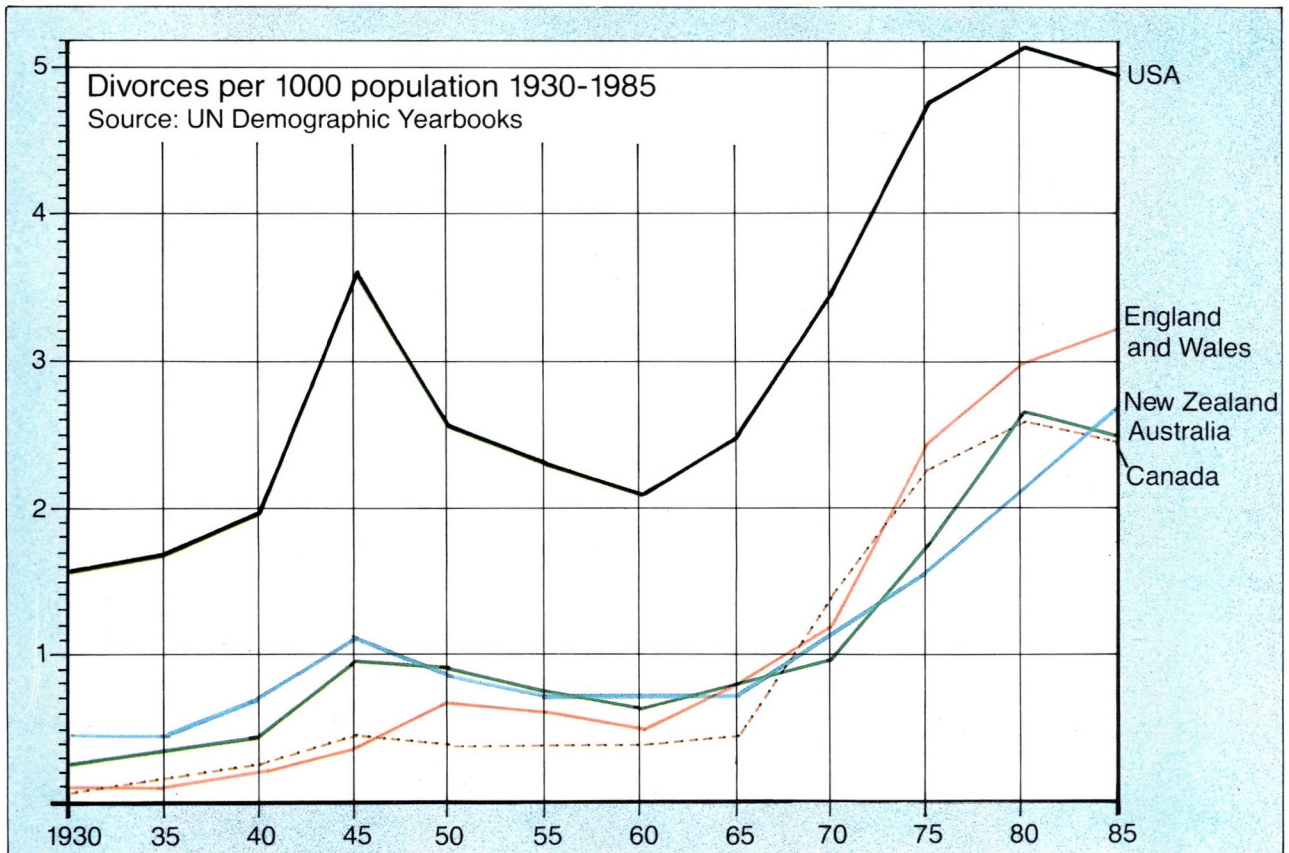

Divorces per 1000 population 1930-1985
Source: UN Demographic Yearbooks

USA
England and Wales
New Zealand
Australia
Canada

For many years, and in most countries, legal grounds for divorce were fault-based (usually adultery, desertion or cruelty). Other grounds included life imprisonment (Sweden), incest (Denmark), constant drunkenness (USSR), or talkativeness (Formosa). One partner was said to be 'guilty' and the other 'innocent'.

Divorce laws also change with the political situation. In the Soviet Union, after the Revolution of 1917, the Communists:

> Permitted every consort to declare that he wanted his marriage to be cancelled. No reasons were to be given. . . . If one of the consorts was absent, he or she was notified [of the divorce] by a postcard. (Nicholas Timasheff, *The Great Retreat,* 1946.)

From 1936, Stalinist family policy almost abolished divorce, but today, grounds for divorce in the USSR include childlessness, marital fault and separation.

During the Chinese Cultural Revolution of 1966 to 1976, in the words of a Chinese lawyer:

> There were almost no officially approved divorces for ordinary people; while on the other hand, a number of people were forced to divorce their so-called revisionist or bourgeois spouses. (*International Journal of Law and the Family,* vol. 1, no. 2, pp 257-8, 1987.)

There are now about half a million divorces a year in China.

Above *During the Cultural Revolution in China the only way of procuring a divorce was by claiming that your partner's views were politically unacceptable. Here people hold up the book that contained the required Revolutionary views.*

In Western countries:
- Three-quarters of divorce actions are by women.
- Average length of marriage to divorce is 7 to 10 years.
- Divorce rate is highest in poor families.
- Over half of divorces involve dependent children.
- Nearly a quarter of divorces (in England) involve at least one partner previously divorced.

Divorce law reform is also brought about by changes in social attitudes. In England there was equality in divorce between men and women only from 1923, and even then:

> Until 1937, adultery was the only type of offence legally recognized as cutting at the root of the marriage relationship and warranting its dissolution. (O. R. McGregor, *Divorce in England,* 1957.)

After 1937, grounds of desertion, cruelty and insanity were added.

Australia had different laws in each state until 1959, after which Commonwealth law allowed divorce on 14 grounds. These included adultery, desertion, five years' separation, cruelty, drunkenness and drug-taking, refusal to consummate, frequent convictions, imprisonment and insanity.

In Muslim countries a man may divorce his wife by repeating three times before witnesses, 'I divorce you'. This Talaq divorce becomes valid after 90 days. Other cultures have their own means of divorce. For instance, in the southern states of the USA, a Pueblo Indian wife could divorce her husband by putting his moccasins outside the door.

Reading the Qur'an. For a devout Muslim, the conditions for a legal divorce are contained in the Qur'an. It was written in about AD 610 and is the infallible word of God for all Muslims.

In the past 20 years, many countries have adopted the principle of irretrievable breakdown of marriage as the only ground of divorce. This can be proved by one year's separation in Australia and New Zealand, by one year's separation, adultery or cruelty in Canada and in Britain by two years' separation, adultery or unreasonable behaviour. In Britain, there are proposals for abolishing the fault grounds and for shortening the required length of separation. In that country the most usual proof of breakdown of their marriage used by wives is their husbands' unreasonable behaviour. Husbands most often give their wives' adultery as proof of breakdown. Both of these proofs provide divorce more quickly than by waiting to complete a two-year separation.

In the USA:

> . . . courts prior to 1970 were often interested in making divorce as difficult to secure as possible, believing that this would force couples to resolve their marital differences. This system, however, tended to increase bitterness and hostility between spouses. . . . In contrast to the adversarial approach to divorce, no-fault legislation maintains that marriages should be terminated without any imputation of guilt or wrongdoing on the part of either spouse . . . (*Divorce*.)

The actress Joan Collins with her lawyer during her divorce case in 1987. A lot of publicity surrounds the divorce of a well-known person, which makes it more difficult for the family to cope with their distress.

A traditional wedding in Japan. In many ways, Japanese society is more conservative than that in countries in the West. Yet, in Japan, a married couple can get a divorce without having to wait for a specified period of separation.

There is no federal divorce law in the USA; every state has its own divorce law. In 1970, California was the first state to introduce 'no-fault' divorce and all other states have now done so.

In China and Japan, divorce is available without delay if both partners agree. The same applies in Sweden if the couple has no children. In Japan, 90 per cent of divorces are by agreement between husband and wife, and in Scotland:

> The truth of the matter is that, under the present law, anybody who wants a divorce can eventually get one. Making divorce less quickly available to some and more quickly available to others is unlikely to affect marriage breakdown rates one way or the other. (Scottish Law Commission, Discussion Paper no. 76, 'The Ground for Divorce', 1988.)

As we can see from this brief survey, divorce law varies greatly from one country to another. However, overall there is a tendency to make divorce easier to acquire. This has increased the number of divorces, but not necessarily the number of married couples who have effectively separated. There remains much controversy over the question of whether easy divorces actually make some marriages less secure.

1 Do you believe that it should be easy to get a divorce? Or do you believe that people should try harder to keep their marriages going? Why?
2 Is it too easy to get married?
3 Do you think it is anyone's fault when a marriage breaks down? Give reasons for your answer.
4 Do you think it is fairer to allow divorce for a 'fault' such as adultery or cruelty, or for a period of separation?

Consequences of divorce

Divorce has many consequences. First of all, divorced people are free to remarry according to the law of their country. There are also changes (often for the worse) in their financial position, housing, health and social status. Divorced people experience many mixed feelings, such as disbelief, anger, guilt, grief, relief and loneliness.

Divorce brings changes in:
● Legal status.
● Housing.
● Social status.
● Income and expenditure.
● Health.
● Feelings.

Financial

Until 1870 in England:

> All property belonging to a married woman on marriage and anything coming to her after marriage, immediately became the property of her husband and she had no right or control over it. (Burgoyne, Ormrod and Richards, *Divorce Matters*, 1987.)

Since then, the law has changed and today joint ownership of the home and equal claims on family assets after divorce are generally accepted.

A father in nineteenth century Britain had total responsibility for the upbringing of his children. If he divorced his wife, she would not be allowed to keep her children.

THE £11m KISS-OFF!

Chat-show king shells out fortune to divorce wife

By HUGH WHITTOW

JOHNNY CARSON'S famous smile had slipped yesterday . . . after he kissed goodbye to £11-million in a divorce deal.

America's chat show king was left speechless when his beautiful third wife Joanna walked off with a record pay-off.

SHE collects £3.5million in cash, **FOUR** homes, **THREE** cars, up to £1.6million alimony, and a priceless Picasso.

HE was jolted by the cost of ending their 10-year marriage . . . even though he is one of the richest men in Hollywood, with assets of £60million.

Beautiful Joanna, 45, battled for three years to clinch the settlement.

Everything was hotly contested . . . right down to Carson's holding of 100 Kruger. . . receiving £30,000

Johnny Carson and Joanna . . . she's celebratng after he agreed to pay out £11million to end their marrage.

Alexis . . . she's his steady girlfriend

WHO GETS WHAT IN CARSON v CARSON

Ending a marriage can involve complex financial arrangements. However, few divorces involve such huge amounts of money, and women are usually the ones who are worse off afterwards.

After a divorce the family income has to support two households. A court may make an order for financial payments from one spouse to the other. It is often difficult to make the money stretch. Until recently one spouse was responsible for the financial support of the other spouse until he or she remarried. Courts in England had to try to:

> . . . place the parties in the financial position in which they would have been if the marriage had not broken down. (Matrimonial Causes Act, 1973.)

Courts in many countries now recommend payments for two or three years only. They can also make financial awards for child support which should continue until the child leaves school. But the money is often not paid. Professor Lenore Weitzman, an American sociologist, wrote in 1985:

> On average, divorced women and the minor children in their households experience a 73 per cent decline in their standard of living in the first year after divorce. Their former husbands, in contrast, experience a 42 per cent rise in their standard of living. (Lenore Weitzman, *The Divorce Revolution*, 1985.)

17

How the Other Half Lives

A divorced woman rings her ex-spouse:

Perhaps you could spare some time to see the children on Saturday... I want to go out.

: THINKS :
Well, it's **all right** for **HIM**...he's got a very **cushy number**....he's not **lonely**.... he's got:
1. GIRL FRIENDS. 2. MONEY 3. A BACHELOR FLAT. 4. NO HOUSEWORK. 5. FREEDOM. 6. UNINTERRUPTED NIGHTS. 7. PARENTAL POWER WITH-OUT RESPONSIBILITY. 8. NO ONE TO THINK ABOUT EXCEPT HIMSELF.
HE HAS, OF COURSE TO PAY MY MAINTENANCE, AND THAT HE MAKES INTO AN ACT OF CHARITY.

Why do you always sound SO **ANGRY?**

: THINKS :
It's **all right** for **HER**...she's got a **cushy** one...........I knacker myself at my job to keep her nice and warm in **my** HOUSE, WITH MY KIDS AND MY DOG AND MY HI-FI AND MY CAR AND MY DAVID HOCKNEY PRINT...AND I DON'T GET ANY THANKS.

© Posy Simmonds 1981

After divorce, ex-wife and ex-husband can have distorted views of how the other half lives. This clever cartoon compares the imagined life-style with the reality.

Some countries have solved the problem. In Australia since 1988,

> . . . maintenance is automatically deducted from the non-custodial parent's wages or salary by his or her employer. The employer then pays that amount to the Registrar of the newly established Child Support Agency. The money is then sent monthly to the custodial parent . . . (Margaret Harrison, Australian Institute of Family Studies, *Family Matters* 21, 1988.)

Other countries, such as Sweden, France and Barbados, have similar arrangements. In small island countries, such as Barbados, it is difficult for a parent to disappear and therefore avoid paying maintenance. In West Germany:

> Mothers and fathers are equally responsible for the maintenance of their children. . . . the custodial parent through caring for the child, the non-custodial parent through the payment of money. [There was] full compliance in about 60 per cent of cases where the mother was the custodial parent. (Wolfgang Voegli, German professor of law, AIFS *Newsletter* 17, January 1987.)

Some wives expect financial support, others do not:

> I deserved it [alimony] because I wasted the best years of my life raising children and being married. (Divorced woman in California, 1985, quoted in *The Divorce Revolution* by Lenore Weitzman.)

> I'm perfectly capable of supporting myself. If you're capable of working, you shouldn't sponge off your ex-husband. (Another divorced woman in California, 1985, quoted in *The Divorce Revolution* by Lenore Weitzman.)

Also in 1985, a judge in California said (of a different woman):

> The best thing for her is to get right out and get a job — earn her own money — and make her own life . . . There are lots of jobs out there, just read the want ads. (*Quoted in The Divorce Revolution* by Lenore Weitzman.)

Various viewpoints come from two divorced women and one divorced man in Australia:

> The money's practically the same, but it goes further now that I'm in charge.

> I live in an old dusty, dingy flat behind my shop which I have to open seven days a week and have had three days off in two years — no holiday of course.

> The woman I now live with also works, and we share all expenses, so my standard of living is higher than before the separation. (All three views quoted in *Breaking Up.*)

The fa'l in the standard of living that often accompanies divorce, naturally affects the children. There is less money to go round, and only one parent to keep an eye on them.

A family living in a shelter for the homeless, in Liverpool. After separation or divorce, the financial consequences often mean that a family is forced to move to a smaller house, or flat. In some cases the family may be forced to rely on the state to provide somewhere to live.

Housing

If husband and wife cannot agree, the court will either award the home to the custodial parent, or instruct that the value of the home be divided between the partners. One partner or both will have to find a new home, which can lead to considerable inconvenience for both partners. This happened in two marriages, in which one husband and one wife give their opinion:

> I lost the lot — my kids, my wife, my home. I had nowhere to go. I drifted from one bedsit to another. What with paying the mortgage so she could enjoy my home, I couldn't afford anywhere decent for myself. Sure the house looks spick and span, but I wish she'd find a job and earn some money of her own, instead of taking all mine.

> The children and I went to live with my parents for a bit. Then David sold the family home and I had to use my half share to find somewhere else. We're unbelievably cramped, and in a poor district.

It is often difficult for a court to make a fair division of property:

> Sex-typing of awards still exists; women continue more often to be awarded the family home and furnishings, whereas husbands are more likely to be awarded the business and the family car. (*Divorce.*)

Health

People whose marriages have broken down are often accident-prone. They have so many problems on their minds that they cannot give all their attention to what they are doing, or to where they are going, so they fall or cut themselves – or worse.

> Controlling for age, premature death rates were higher for divorced men and women than for married persons, with differences being significantly greater for men than for women. (US National Center for Health Statistics, 1985.)

> Compared with married men, the divorced male has double the risk of suffering a fatal stroke, four times the risk of suicide and seven times the risk of dying from cirrhosis of the liver. (American actuarial statistics, *Intercity*, February, 1989.)

While emotional problems are initially more severe for men, women may experience more long-term divorce distress. As one English divorced woman put it:

> I stayed in a state of shock, I would say, for months. Over the next six months I lost two and a half stone – a lot of weight, quickly. No appetite. No sleep. It's very common I'm told. (Quoted in Catherine Itzin, *Splitting Up*, 1980.)

A sudden separation can leave people in a state of shock, particularly when someone has been deserted by his or her partner.

Sometimes there is an improvement in health, as in the case of this divorced woman:

> I was released from the fear of what he'd do to me when he came home. I used to dread hearing his key in the lock. After years of misery, I felt tremendous relief that at last I'd got rid of him. No more valium, no more smoking, no more sleepless nights. (Mitchell[2].)

Social status

There used to be great social stigma attached to divorce.

> It was not until 1887 that Queen Victoria would allow even the innocent party to a divorce-suit to attend her court. . . . A leading statesman could be ruined politically by a charge of adultery. (R.C.K. Ensor, *England 1870-1914*, 1936.)
> Divorce remained a serious barrier in public life and, in Court circles, an insuperable one. . . . The Conservative Party maintained a ban on divorce until after the Second World War. (A.J.P. Taylor, *English History 1914-1945*, 1965.)
> A recently appointed headmaster was sacked by the school's governors when they found out that he had been divorced. True, it was a Catholic school. (Patricia Goldacre, *Times Educational Supplement*, 8 May, 1981.)

In recent years, the stigma that was previously associated with divorce has faded and a divorce is no longer seen as a mark of failure. Even so, social status is still affected by divorce. A divorced person is no longer half of a couple. This may change relationships with friends, especially other couples.

For women who have suffered physical abuse from their husbands, a separation can constitute an escape from danger.

> Old friends do not wish to know you. You have become something of an embarrassment to them, or to their husbands. (*Breaking Up.*)

Like a road accident or a burglary, divorce is often seen as something that happens to other people.

> When I first embarked upon this study . . . I imagined that in the permissive climate of the present day a divorcee would be as acceptable a part of the social scene as the married, the widowed and the single. But I soon learnt, from a variety of sources, that stigma was very much a part of the divorcee's experience. (Nicky Hart, *When Marriage Ends,* 1976.)

Nicky Hart was told by two divorcees:

> Well, I suppose I had thought about it before. I mean, I had friends who had split up. But I never seriously thought that something like that would happen to us.

> Widowed people get treated with sympathy and respect; there is a very definite stigma still attached to the divorced and separated.

A divorce or separation may relieve a lot of pent up anger and frustration, allowing both partners to live their lives in the way they choose.

Feelings

People have mixed and intense feelings about their divorce. Carol, a Scottish divorced woman, said in 1986:

> I was so thankful to be rid of him, and yet I missed him. . . . I didn't want to go on living with him, but now I wish he'd come back. (Mitchell[2].)

Some feel disbelief, as this divorced man testified:

> It was like being hit with a sledge-hammer when she walked out on me. I should have expected it because she gave plenty of warning. (Mitchell[1].)

Many have strong feelings of anger:

> The most common reaction to marital breakdown is anger, which is actually a disguise for deep disappointment and anxiety at the threat of being deserted and losing a loved one. (B. and G. Oberg, *I'm Leaving,* 1982.)

Many divorced people feel a great sense of guilt:

> The other person in the relationship, the one who has left, and is cast as an executioner, is caught by their sense of guilt and often dares not show their grief in case people say 'What do you mean? If you are unhappy you can always go back'. (*I'm Leaving.*)

'Divorce is like death without the dignity', was the view of one Scottish divorcee. Coming to terms with the grief of a separation is very important:

Feelings about divorce include:
- Disbelief.
- Guilt.
- Relief.
- Anger.
- Grief.
- Loneliness.

24

> Grief is an important feature in divorce. . . . It is quite acceptable to be unhappy and despairing if someone close to us dies. With separation it is the opposite. Grieving for someone who has left home and family may be thought, even by one's nearest and dearest, a thoroughly wrong action. . . . People who lose a loved one to another person are forced to contain their grief and only express anger and bitterness. (*I'm Leaving.*)

As well as guilt and grief, for many there are feelings of relief and happiness at the ending of an unwanted marriage:

> I wanted to get ahead. I wanted freedom. I discovered I did not want to be married. (*Breaking Up.*)

> I bought a new car and my own TV set and was able to watch my choice of TV programme. I started going out occasionally instead of waiting for the rare occasions when he would take me anywhere. (Australian divorcee, quoted in *Breaking Up.*)

After separation, loneliness can become a major problem:

> There is no one to listen to you, no one to talk to, no one to laugh with or to commiserate with. There is no one with whom to share the little events of the day, and not even anyone to argue with. (Mitchell[2].)

> I thought the walls were closing in on me, as I listened to the silence. (Mitchell[2].)

The American psychologist, Judith Wallerstein, sums up the general difficulties faced by many divorcing couples:

> Divorce is not a more 'normal' experience simply because so many people have been touched by it. (*Second Chances*, 1989.)

> *1 Do you believe that a husband should have to support his wife financially after divorce? Give your reasons.*
> *2 Why is it difficult to make the money stretch after separation? Can you think of any solutions?*
> *3 Why should marriage breakdown affect people's health?*
> *4 Should divorced families be treated differently from two-parent families?*

Life alone, without a partner, can be desperately lonely and miserable.

Divorce and children

Although a husband and wife might be divorced from each other, nothing can change the fact that they will always be father and mother to their children. This continues to be true even if children lose touch with one parent, and even if one parent (or both) remarries. However, there will be changes for the children, who will probably live with one parent.

Until the nineteenth century, children were looked on as the property of the father. Custody was sometimes awarded to mothers, but never to an adulterous mother. By the early twentieth century, children of 'tender years' (under school age) were thought to be better off living with their mothers.

> A child of this age [three] . . . ought to be with the mother, if other things are equal. (English judge, *Family Law*, vol 14, 1983.)

Nowadays, in the majority of divorcing families, parents make their own arrangements, although maternal custody remains the preferred pattern for most mothers and fathers.

ADOLPH ZUKOR & JESSE L. LASKY present
CLARA BOW and ESTHER RALSTON
in
"**CHILDREN** OF **DIVORCE**"
with
Gary Cooper, Einar Hanson and Norman Trevor
A Frank Lloyd Production
From the novel by Owen Johnson

This film of 1927 focused on what was then a relatively rare phenomenon. Notice that these girls are depicted as coming from a wealthy family. At that time, only the well-off would have been able to afford an official divorce.

In contrast to Children of Divorce *the film* Kramer vs Kramer *(1979) portrayed a realistic image of the problems faced by a child whose parents are divorced. The film highlighted the bewilderment and despair felt by the child when his mother left home, and the difficulties involved when the parents contest custody of the child.*

When parents cannot agree, the court can ask for an investigation into the children's welfare. Some parents appreciate this, but others do not. In the view of an English divorced woman:

> It proved a helpful and clarifying experience. Both welfare officers were tactful and sensitive. Going over the history was helpful. I think we talked about things we might otherwise have avoided.(Clulow and Vincent, *In The Child's Best Interests?*, 1987.)

But:

> Parents have enough problems to sort out about broken marriages without bringing the children into it. (Scottish divorced woman, 1985, Mitchell[3].)

In the small percentage of divorces where there is a legal dispute over custody of the children, it is now awarded according to 'the best interests of the child'. This can be difficult to decide in a law court:

> Judges find it difficult to decide in other-than-clear custody cases, so they declare women to be the natural custodians knowing that this may be wrong, but in the absence of sufficient time it will be safer to decide in this manner. (Dr Donald Cramer, member of West German organization of non-custodial fathers, *ACCESS*, vol. 2, no. 1, February, 1986.)

27

Opinions differ over the suitability of fathers to look after their children:

> These young fathers really want to keep the children — and they have the ability and financial resources to do it. (Californian attorney in 1975, Lenore Weitzman, *The Divorce Revolution*.)

> Generally speaking, a man is asking for custody to punish his spouse. He feels that he can hurt his wife the most by trying to take the kids away from her. (Another Californian attorney in 1975, Lenore Weitzman, *The Divorce Revolution*.)

> He didn't really want the children. It was just his pride. He was determined that I shouldn't have them. He didn't seem to mind how much they suffered, so long as I was suffering. (English mother of two children kidnapped by their Algerian father, the *Guardian*, 9 July, 1987.)

> Even though the law says there isn't a presumption [in favour of mother custody] I still think mothers make better mothers. (Los Angeles judge in 1975, Lenore Weitzman, *The Divorce Revolution*.)

An English judge who removed a two-and-a-half year old girl from her father who had raised her single-handed from the age of nine months, explained his action by stating that:

> A man's brain should be used for working and not for turning himself into a mother. (The *Guardian*, 27 September, 1979.)

Above *Fathers are nowadays far more involved in their children's lives than they used to be and are often well able to 'mother' their children.*

Other countries have been slower to consider whether children should live with their mothers. Before the Second World War, Japanese mothers did not have any right to custody of their children. Even up to about 1969, divorced fathers nearly always looked after their children. In Japan, many people believed that women were inferior to men and would not be capable of looking after children or of seeing that they were educated. In Muslim countries and in Greece, children are still seen as the father's property.

However, in most countries both parents have the right to bring up their children, whoever has custody. Since 1980, the concept of joint custody has spread. This might mean that the children have two homes, dividing their time between two parents. Or it might mean that they live with one parent while the other has the right to be closely involved in their lives.

A divorce court has the power to award a parent 'reasonable access' ('visitation' in the USA) to a child, or can specify, say, every second Saturday, and half of each school holiday. Most courts take the view that it is in the interests of a child to retain contact with both of his or her parents.

This Arab father has a child whose mother is European. If the parents separate, the child might have difficulties in adjusting between homes in two different cultures.

29

However, in many divorces the parents make their own arrangements for access. After divorce, between a third and a half of children soon lose touch with one parent. According to recent research in Australia:

> Many departing parents probably have no idea how much they are still needed in the lives of their children. (Dunlop and Burns, *'Don't Feel the World is Caving In'*, 1988.)

Professional opinions differ as to whether children should continue to see both parents:

> Once it is determined who will be the custodial parent, it is that parent, not the court, who must decide under what conditions he or she wishes to raise the child. Thus, the non-custodial parent should have no legally enforceable right to visit the child, and the custodial parent should have the right to decide whether it is desirable for the child to have such visits. (Goldstein, Freud and Solnit, American therapists, *Beyond the Best Interests of the Child*, 1973.)

> Divorcing parents should be encouraged and helped to shape post-divorce arrangements which permit and foster continuity in the children's relations with both parents. (Wallerstein and Kelly, *Surviving the Breakup*, 1980.)

Parents and children have to learn to say 'Hello' and 'Goodbye' to each other, when the children leave one parent in order to visit the other.

A day out at the fair. Children may realize that they are competing for their parents' affection, and play one off against the other. This boy asks his mother for some money to spend, saying that his father did not give him any.

> Your child is not the one who got the divorce and should neither have to lose contact with one parent as a result of it, nor be burdened, especially as he gets older, with an inflexible visitation schedule. (Goldstein and Solnit, *Divorce & Your Child*, 1984.)

Some Scottish parents' views include:

> They knew I didn't like it [access] and I'm sure they never saw their mother. I don't believe in access. Children don't know which way they're going if they have access. (Father with custody of four children, 1985, Mitchell[3].)

> I had to grit my teeth and tell Caroline where my husband would meet her. I didn't want anything to do with him. But it wasn't Caroline's fault that I hated him for what he'd done. He was still her father. (Mitchell[3].)

> He hadn't done much with them for quite a time. Suddenly to go out with this family you don't really know can be difficult. During the marriage, my husband didn't want to keep on being a father to his children, and then I expected him to take on an unaccustomed role of father. (Mitchell[3].)

The love of grandparents (and, in this case, of a great grandmother) is extremely important to children and continues if the parents separate.

As the last mother realized, access is an artificial situation where a child usually sees a parent by appointment. Careful planning is necessary to make meetings enjoyable for the child and the parent. Children have views about access too:

> It seemed natural to go out with him. It was coming home again that was difficult. We thought Dad wanted to stay when he brought us home. (Girl, 1985, Mitchell[3].)

> It's as if only my body came back and my soul was still at Daddy's. (Swedish boy, tearful on returning from a visit to his father, 1982, quoted in *I'm Leaving.*)

> My Mum never said anything about visiting my Dad. I would have wanted to see him. (Boy, 1985, Mitchell[3].)

By losing touch with one parent, a child can also lose grandparents and other relatives:

> Our son was divorced nine months ago and our daughter-in-law has taken the children and does not let us see them. She sent back their birthday presents. (Letter from grandparents to a national magazine, 1986.)

There are some self-help organizations for such grandparents, but they cannot help the children.

Most parents find it difficult to tell their children what is happening. Some are too upset to explain anything.

> They never seemed to question anything at the time, so I thought it best to let things just go on. It might have upset them otherwise. (Father, quoted in Mervyn Murch, *Justice and Welfare in Divorce*, 1980.)

> I never tell Derek anything that's going on, ever. He's never heard anything, because if they hear snatches they get hold of the wrong end of the stick. (Divorced mother, 1987, *In The Child's Best Interests?*)

> I told the children I'd stopped loving their Dad and wanted to get away from him. (Mother, 1985, Mitchell[3].)

Children, especially younger ones, do not always understand the word 'divorce'. Some think it means they will not be allowed to see one parent ever again, and of course that is not true.

Children can be aware that their parents are not getting on together, but dare not believe that the family might split up. Some children do not realize that their parents have split up permanently.

> I never really knew. Mum told me and I was really mad with her. I said, 'You could have told me something was going on.' (Teenage girl, 1988, *'Don't Feel the World is Caving In'.*)

> **In Western countries:**
> In the USA 40-50 per cent, in Britain 20 per cent and in Australia 16 per cent of children will probably have divorced parents before leaving school. Some will experience several parental divorces. Fewer than 10 per cent of divorces involve court custody disputes.

It can be difficult for children to understand why their parents will not stay together, especially just after a visit by the non-custodial parent.

33

> It didn't occur to me they'd split up for good because they still saw each other all the time. (Girl, 1985, Mitchell[3].)
> It's funny to think you have a close-knit family, no — not think, but KNOW you have — and then find your parents want to separate. (Boy, 1985, Mitchell[3].)

Parents and children often do not understand each other.

> My Mum didn't understand how I felt. She was too busy being angry. (Girl, 1985, Mitchell[3].)
> I thought it was rotten of my Mum to divorce my Dad. I felt sorry for Dad because he had nobody. (Girl, Mitchell[3].)
> Children can understand a lot more about their parents than their parents think they can. (Ten-year-old girl, BBC TV, 1988.)

School can be helpful or hurtful:

> I thought I was the only one in the world that didn't have a Dad, but when I got to secondary school I realized there were quite a few like me and I didn't feel so bad. (Girl, 1985, McCredie and Horrox, *Voices in the Dark*.)

Teenagers may feel some comfort from friends who have also experienced their parents' separation.

> I've kept it mainly to myself. Some kids in the form are so rotten they'd rip you to pieces on it. (Fifteen-year-old boy, 1988, *'Don't Feel the World is Caving In'.*)

> At school, I just sat there and couldn't think about anything except my parents and family. After a while the teachers stopped getting on at me. I suppose someone must have told them. (Boy, Mitchell[3].)

Research into a cross-section of divorced families showed:

> - Only one-third of parents gave children some information.
>   - Only half of children had been conscious of parental conflict.
>   - Only one child in ten had been unhappy before separation.
>   - One-third of children immediately lost touch with one parent.
>   - Another third lost touch within five years. (Mitchell[3].)

Opinions differ about whether children are better or worse off when their parents split up. For many years people believed that unhappy parents should stick together for the sake of the children. But in recent years there has been a growing belief by adults that children are better off in a separated family than in an unhappy home. Some, however, do not agree with this:

Parents often fail to understand how much their arguments can upset their children.

Advice to parents
- Talk to your children.
- Tell them you are both still their parents.
- Tell them divorce is not their fault.
- Help them to keep in touch with both of you.
- Make as few changes in their routine as possible.

Children can feel very lonely at school if their friends do not understand how unhappy they are about their family life.

> People who get divorced want to think they are doing the best thing for their children. Actually they are doing the best thing for themselves. They simply don't want to deal with the issue of the children because they feel guilty. (Jill Krementz, the *Sunday Telegraph,* 3 November, 1985.)

Many children want their parents to stay together:

> The unconscious aim of the one-parent children was always the same: to preserve at all costs the idea that both parents were still looking after them. (French college professor, 1985, see *ACCESS,* February 1986, vol. 2, no. 1.)

Other children are happier when their parents split up:

> My parents divorced when I was eleven years of age and for me and my brothers it was a godsend. (Teenager, in Vivekanandra and Nicholson, *Picking Up the Pieces,* 1987.)

Some children just accept the inevitable:

> About divorce, in the long run it's good; in the short range it isn't. (Twelve-year-old boy, 1980, *Surviving the Breakup.*)

> On no account stay together for the sake of the children but, having agreed to separate, parents should try to forget their personal feelings and concentrate on the children. (Girl, 1985, Mitchell[3].)

Whatever might happen to children whose parents divorce, they will have to make many adjustments:

> Where children are involved in divorce cases there are no ideal situations or perfect solutions; there will always be loss for someone, there will always be hard and painful feelings. (*I'm Leaving.*)

> For the children of divorce, growing up is unquestionably harder every step of the way. (*Second Chances.*)

---

1 Do you think fathers and mothers are equally capable of looking after their children after divorce?
2 Do you think that children should continue to see both parents after divorce? Give some reasons for your answer.
3 Describe how life might change for a child after divorce.
4 How can grandparents help after a divorce?

5

Help

When a marriage breaks down, help is needed for many of the consequences described in chapter three. This can be professional (legal, medical or counselling) or informal support.

In some countries, divorce can be obtained without any legal assistance, especially if there are no dependent children and no financial claims from one spouse to the other. But nevertheless it is usually wise to consult a lawyer.

> The attorney is probably in the most strategic position of all professionals in contact with divorcing families to help clients avoid some of the common problems related to the divorce process. (Divorce.)

Research shows that more wives than husbands consult their doctor when their marriage breaks down. They suffer from 'nerves', sleeplessness, eating problems, heavy drinking or generally feeling unwell. Many people are prescribed tranquillizers, but some are reluctant to take them.

A counsellor or mediator can help a couple to talk about their feelings and to understand each other's point of view. Here, models pose for the camera, in real life the child would not be present at a meeting between parents and counsellor.

> I had to go to the doctor when I found I was living off my nerves. (Ex-wife, 1981, Mitchell[1].)

> My doctor was a bit too willing to carry on prescribing. I thought I could get repeat prescriptions [for tranquillizers] too easily. (Ex-wife, 1981, Mitchell[1].)

There are many specialist agencies for separating couples and also self-help groups such as Gingerbread in the UK, and Parents Without Partners in the USA. Marriage counsellors help people to understand themselves and each other — they are not marriage menders.

Family conciliation or mediation services help couples to deal with difficulties arising from the breakup of their relationship, particularly problems relating to children. Such services can be attached to divorce courts (in Australia, New Zealand and some places in the USA and Britain) or they can be independent. In Australia and California, couples who cannot agree about arrangements for their children must talk to a counsellor or mediator at the court. However, research shows that, on the whole, family and friends give more support than professionals.

When a marriage ends, people turn most often to their mothers for comfort and support, and to their lawyers for legal advice. Family and friends are more easily available than professional counsellors.

A cross-section of divorced people in the UK were helped by (in percentage):

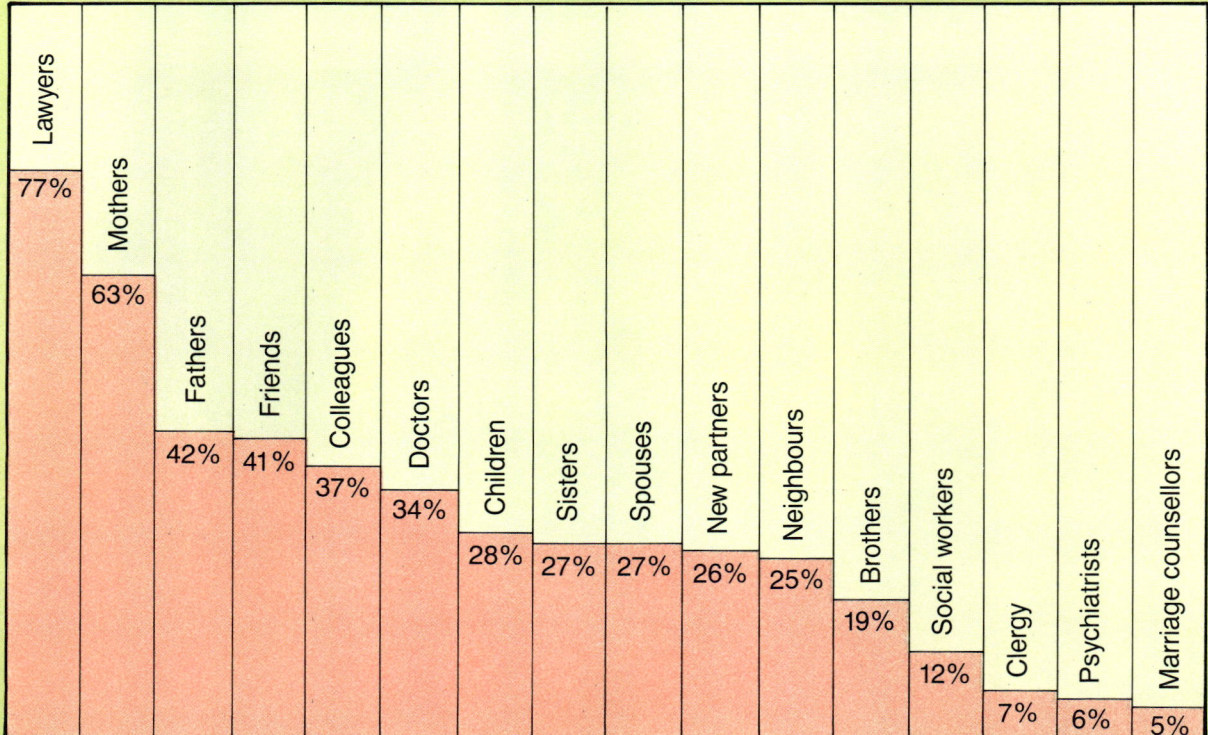

	Percentage
Lawyers	77%
Mothers	63%
Fathers	42%
Friends	41%
Colleagues	37%
Doctors	34%
Children	28%
Sisters	27%
Spouses	27%
New partners	26%
Neighbours	25%
Brothers	19%
Social workers	12%
Clergy	7%
Psychiatrists	6%
Marriage counsellors	5%

Talking through a problem with friends can help people to find their own solutions.

> The help and support that family, friends and neighbours give to each other is so much taken for granted that it often hardly enters into the discussion of the provision of social services. (Wolfenden Committee on The Future of Voluntary Organizations, 1978.)

Parents' support can be very important; as one Scottish divorced woman said of her parents:

> It was very comforting to be with them, and they were very sympathetic. (Mitchell[1].)

But some parents do not understand:

> My parents keep putting pressure on me to return to my wife. They can't understand that it's out of the question. The trouble is, I tried not to let them know just how bad it was, so the split came as a shock to them. (Schoolteacher, 1986, Mitchell[2].)

Some friends are very helpful, but some are not:

> All my friends have helped by sitting and listening. I went on and on about it at first. (Scottish divorced woman, 1981, Mitchell[1].)

> Friends are afraid that they will have to take sides; neighbours think it is none of their business. . . . When a man and woman divorce, many people tend to act as if they believe it might be contagious. (*Second Chances.*)

There are very few services available to children of divorcing parents:

> Existing services for children are grossly inadequate. . . . Children appear to be in particular need of divorce-related support services, yet existing services tend to be in a state of development and are not widely available. (*Divorce.*)

---

1 Can you say why it might be wise to consult a lawyer?
2 Why do people find it difficult to know what to say to friends who separate or divorce?
3 What sort of help do you think would be useful for children whose parents split up?

6

Remarriage

The law everywhere allows a divorced person to remarry. But some Churches discourage remarriage. A divorced Catholic cannot be remarried in a Catholic church because they are still considered to be married to the first spouse. A Catholic whose first marriage was valid and who remarried after divorce, is not allowed to receive communion. Similarly, some Protestant Churches are reluctant to remarry divorced people.

> 'The news that the hitherto respected Foreign Secretary has entered into a so-called "marriage" with the Prime Minister's niece during the lifetime of his own wife has come as an outrageous shock to Christian sentiment throughout the land,' wrote a Rural Dean of the Church of England in his parish magazine when Anthony Eden (later Prime Minister) married Clarissa Churchill in 1952. (Quoted by A.P. Herbert in *The Right to Marry,* 1954.)

However, attitudes within most Protestant Churches are now more tolerant than they used to be.

In Britain:
- 70-80 per cent of divorced people remarry.
- One in three marriages involve one divorced partner.
- One in six marriages involve two divorced partners.
- Divorced women who remarry are twice as likely to divorce as women in a first marriage.
- Divorced men who remarry are one-and-a-half times as likely to divorce as men in a first marriage.
- One quarter of divorces are re-divorces for one or both partners.

British Prime Minister Anthony Eden seen with his wife Clarissa, returning from their honeymoon, in 1952. Eden faced public criticism for remarrying after his divorce, but his political career was not curtailed, as it would have been a generation earlier.

This farmer in Aswan, Egypt, lives with his two wives (shown here) and his six children.

In Muslim countries, polygamy is allowed, but few Muslim men can afford to have more than one wife at a time. Any who have the maximum of four wives can divorce one in order to marry a fifth.

> I have four wives as the Prophet allows. . . . I have married and divorced a hundred, and if God wills I shall marry and divorce many more. (King Ibn Saud of Arabia, in 1917, quoted in H. C. Armstrong, *Lord of Arabia,* 1924.)

Remarriage was described by Dr Samuel Johnson in 1770 as 'the triumph of hope over experience'. A more pessimistic comment was voiced by the psychoanalyst Edmund Bergler, in 1948:

> The chances of finding conscious happiness in the next marriage are exactly zero . . . . The second, third and nth marriages are but repetitions of previous experiences. (*Divorce Won't Help.*)

You might think 'once bitten, twice shy' would apply to divorced people, who would not be keen to risk another marriage:

> On the face of it, we would expect newly separated or divorced people to be reluctant candidates for new partnerships; they have found marriage such a painful, destructive and embittering experience . . . (Jacqueline Burgoyne, English sociologist, *Breaking Even,* 1984.)

However, the majority of divorced people do remarry, especially younger ones.

> Nothing restores adult self-esteem and happiness after divorce as quickly and thoroughly as a love affair or a successful second marriage. (*Second Chances.*)

> I don't think any woman can be content without a husband beside her. (Australian divorced woman, 1980, *Breaking Up.*)

There are pitfalls in second marriages that are not present in first marriages, and a second marriage is more likely to end in divorce than a first marriage:

> Am I alone in my bitter hatred of my husband's first wife? (*Stepfamily Newsletter,* winter 1986.)

> There is a general belief that people remarry someone very similar to their first partner, but remarrieds usually profess the opposite — they need to demonstrate to themselves and everyone else that choice number one was an error of judgement, therefore choice number two has to appear to be very different. (Helen Franks, *Remarriage,* 1988.)

> Second wives find out they are like first wives when things go wrong. What is his response when you burn the toast or ruin his shirt? 'You are as bad as my ex-wife.' (Maggie Drummond, *How to Survive as a Second Wife,* 1981.)

> The high failure rate of second marriages is serious and often devastating because it reinforces the first failure many times over. (*Second Chances.*)

Remarriage brings many changes for children, particularly the relationship with their parent's new partner. For instance:

> Stepfamilies are confronted by several myths; first that they are the same as first families, second that love will happen easily and instantly in the new family, and most difficult of all — the myth of the cruel step-parent. (The National Stepfamily Association, *Taking Steps,* 1984.)

> From the child's point of view, a stepfather is like a main character in a play who arrives in the middle of the second act. (*Second Chances.*)

Children themselves have opinions about step-parents:

> You can't just change fathers like that, can you? (A little boy.)

> My Mum offered not to get married if I didn't want it. But she was so happy, I couldn't say no, so I pretended it was all right. (Teenage girl, 1985, Mitchell[3].)

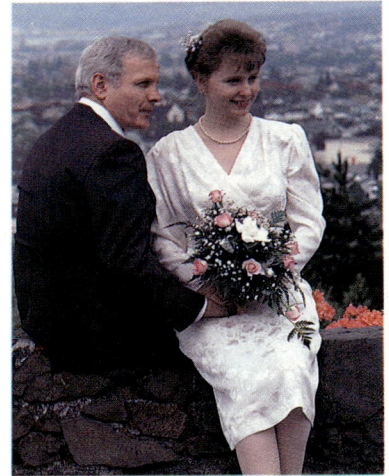

Above *Many divorced people do remarry, though the ceremony for a second marriage is often more relaxed and informal.*

On remarriage, the new family might include:
- Her, his and their children.
- Visits from his or her children.
- Four sets of grandparents.
- Two different surnames.

> It felt good living with him. Mum could have coped on her own, but having a father made life an awful lot easier. (Teenage boy, 1985, Mitchell[3].)

Research shows that children are more likely to get on well with step-parents if they have a good relationship with both of their own parents.

> Karen, aged three, refused to greet her mother's fiancé. 'You're not my daddy,' she said tartly. Only after the child was reassured that the man knew that she had a daddy and wanted additionally to be her friend did the child permit the conversation to proceed. (Californian girl, 1980, in *Surviving the Breakup*.)

<table>
<tr><td>

1   List some advantages and disadvantages of remarriage, for adults and for children.
2   Why can a remarriage have more difficulties than a first marriage?
3   Describe some of the changes for children when a divorced parent remarries.

</td></tr>
</table>

In legends and stories, step-parents and stepfamilies are almost always evil and mean. For instance, here we see a production of the popular pantomime 'Cinderella', where the heroine is mistreated by her cruel stepfather and stepsisters (pictured here).

43

7

Conclusion

After rising rapidly during the 1960s and 1970s, the number of divorces has remained fairly steady in some countries for the past few years. It is possible therefore that the divorce rate has reached its peak.

Couples marrying today must be more aware of the risk of divorce than their parents or grandparents were. But the knowledge of that risk does not seem to stop people from getting married. Marriage is still popular, and over 90 per cent of people marry at least once. They either believe that their marriage will be happy ever after, or they think that they could escape from an unhappy marriage by divorcing. Those two beliefs are illustrated by these comments from young people planning marriage:

> My parents were divorced and I'm determined not to do the same. I wouldn't want to put any child of mine through what I went through. We'll have to work hard at our marriage.

> I suppose if it doesn't work out, we can just get divorced without any difficulty. It's worth a try.

Marriage is still popular, and is still, usually, a positive step for both partners.

In Western countries, many couples now live together without marrying. For some of them, this is a preliminary stage before marriage. Other couples decide not to marry, even when they are legally free to do so, especially in Scandinavian countries. In the past, cohabitation was much less common and was generally frowned on as 'living in sin'; children of unmarried parents often suffered from the stigma of illegitimacy.

If the number of those who cohabit without marriage increases, then their separations will not be marked by divorce, and the divorce rate will appear to decrease. When there is no marriage, there can be no divorce: but there would still be informal separations, with or without children. We can conclude that either:

> Divorce is a wrenching experience for many adults and almost all children. It is almost always more devastating for children than for their parents. (*Second Chances.*)

or:

> The increase of divorce is, in reality, a healthy sign proving, as it does, that people have become less tolerant of evils which were once endured and for which divorce is the only remedy. (William Carson, *The Marriage Revolt,* 1915.)

Finally, we should remember that the majority of marriages do not end in divorce.

> 1 **Has this book changed your ideas about divorce? If so, how?**
> 2 **What advice or help would you give to a divorcing family?**

Glossary

Access Arrangements for a child to meet or visit his or her parent who no longer lives with the family; sometimes called 'contact', or 'visitation'.

Adultery Sexual intercourse between a married person and someone to whom he or she is not married.

Alimony Financial payments from one spouse to the other spouse and the children.

Annulment Declaration by Church or law court that a marriage was not valid.

Attorney Lawyer.

Celibate Living without a sexual relationship.

Cohabit To live together with someone. The word usually refers to men and women who live together, but who are not married to each other.

Consort Old-fashioned word for husband or wife.

Consummate To make a marriage legally complete, by having sexual intercourse.

Custody The legal right of one parent (or both) to make major decisions for a child, on subjects such as education. Often used to mean the day-to-day care of a child by one parent or both. Sometimes called 'residence'.

Illegitimate A child whose parents are not married to each other.

Migratory divorce A divorce obtained by going to live in another state or another country, where divorce is more easily obtainable.

Perjury Giving false evidence in court when under oath to speak the truth.

Polygamy Having more than one marriage partner.

Referendum An opportunity for the public to vote on an important matter.

Spouse Husband or wife.

Further information

You can contact these organizations to find out more about the issues covered in this book.

Academy of Family Mediators, P.O. Box 4686, Greenwich, CT 06830, USA.

Association of Family and Conciliation Courts, OHSU – Psychiatry GH 149, 3181 S.W. Sam Jackson Park, Portland, Oregon 97201, USA.

Australian Institute of Family Studies, 300 Queen Street, Melbourne 3000, Victoria, Australia.

Family Mediation Canada, c/o 123 Woolwich Street, Guelph, Ontario NIH 3V1, Canada.

National Family Conciliation Council, 34 Milton Road, Swindon SN1 5JA, England.

National Marriage Guidance Council of Australia, Suite 8, 696 High Street, East Kew, Victoria 3102, Australia.

National Marriage Guidance Council of New Zealand, Private Bag, Wellington, New Zealand.

Relate (National Marriage Guidance), Little Church Street, Rugby CV21 3AP, England.

Scottish Association of Family Conciliation Services, 127 Rose Street, South Lane, Edinburgh EH2 5BB, Scotland.

Scottish Marriage Guidance Council, 26 Frederick Street, Edinburgh EH2 2JR, Scotland.

Further reading

References in the text to titles by Ann Mitchell:

1 *Someone To Turn To* (Aberdeen University Press, 1981)
2 *Coping with Separation and Divorce* (Chambers, 1986)
3 *Children in the Middle* (Tavistock Publications, 1985)

For teenagers

Blume, Judy *It's Not the End of the World* (Piccolo, 1979)
Fine, Anne *Madame Doubtfire* (Hamish Hamilton, 1987)
Mitchell, Ann *When Parents Split Up* (Chambers, 1986) (Distributed in the USA and Australia by Cambridge University Press)
Robson, Bonnie *My Parents Are Divorced Too* (Dorset Publishing Inc., 1979)

For teachers

Burns, Ailsa *Breaking Up* (Thomas Nelson, 1980)
Cox, Kathleen and Desforges, Martin *Divorce and the School* (Methuen, 1987)
Divorce Pack of informative leaflets for adults and children (The Children's Society, Edward Rudolf House, Margery Street, London WC1X 0JL, England, 1988)
Dunlop, Rosemary and Burns, Ailsa *'Don't Feel the World is Caving In'* (Australian Institute of Family Studies, Melbourne, 1988)
Levinger, George and Moles, Oliver (eds) *Divorce and Separation* (Basic Books, 1979)
Mitchell, Ann *Children in the Middle* (Tavistock Publications, 1985)
Price, Sharon and McKenry, Patrick *Divorce* (Sage Publications, 1988)
Wallerstein, Judith and Blakeslee, Sandra *Second Chances* (Ticknor & Fields, 1989)
Wallerstein, Judith and Kelly, Joan *Surviving the Breakup* (Basic Books, 1980)

Acknowledgements

The publishers have attempted to contact all copyright holders of the quotations in this title, and apologise if there have been any oversights.

The publishers gratefully acknowledge permission from the following to reproduce extracts from copyright material: Artlook Books, *ACCESS*, vol. 2, no.1, February 1986; Australian Institute of Family Studies: 1) article by Margaret Harrison in *Newsletter* no.21; 2) article by Wolfgang Voegli in *Newsletter* no.17; 3) *'Don't Feel the World is Caving In'*, Dunlop and Burns, 1988; Basil Blackwell, *Surviving The Breakup*, Wallerstein and Kelly, 1980; The Bodley Head and Anthony Sheil Associates, *Remarriage*, Helen Franks, 1988; Anthony Clare, *Lovelaw*, 1986; EP Dutton, *The Great Retreat*, Nicolas Timasheff, 1946; The Free Press, *The Divorce Revolution*, Dr Lenore Weitzman, 1985; Heinemann Ltd, *Divorce in England*, OR McGregor, 1957; The National Step Family Association, *Taking Steps*, 1984; Thomas Nelson, *Breaking Up*, Professor Ailsa Burns, 1980; Jill Norman & Hobhouse Ltd, *I'm Leaving*, Bente and Gunnar Oberg, 1982; the *Observer*, article by Katharine Whitehorn, 27 March 1988; Oxford University Press: 1) *English History 1914–1945*, AJP Taylor, 1965; 2) *England 1870–1914*, RCK Ensor, 1936; Penguin Books Ltd: 1) *Divorce Matters*, Burgoyne, Ormrod and Richards, 1987; 2) *Breaking Even*, Jacqueline Burgoyne 1984; Robson Books, *How to Survive as a Second Wife*, Maggie Drummond 1981; Sage Publications Ltd, *Divorce*, Sharon S Price and Patrick C McKenry, 1988; the *Sunday Telegraph*, article 3 November, 1985; Sweet & Maxwell, *Justice and Welfare in Divorce*, Mervyn Murch, 1980; Tavistock Publications, *In the Child's Best Interests?*, Christopher Clulow and Christopher Vincent, 1987; Ticknor & Fields, *Second Chances*, Dr Judith Wallerstein, 1989; *The Times Educational Supplement*, article by Patricia Goldacre, 8 May 1981; Unwin Hyman Ltd: 1) *Voices in the Dark*, McCredie and Horrox, 1985; 2) *The Subversive Family*, Ferdinand Mount, 1983; 3) *Picking Up the Pieces*, Vivekanandra and Nicholson, 1987; Virago Press, *Splitting Up*, Catherine Itzin, 1980; Yale University Press, *Divorce and Your Child*, Goldstein and Solnit, 1984.

The publishers would like to thank the following for providing the illustrations in this book: Chapel Studios 15, 42; Donald Cooper/Photostage 43; Mary Evans 8, 10, 16, 26; John Frost Historical Newspapers 7, 17; Sally & Richard Greenhill 12, 21, 24, 36, 39; Kobal Collection 27; Mansell Collection 4; Christine Osborne 5, 13, 29, 41; Photo Co-op 35, 45 (Gina Glover, both); Photo Research International 22, 32, 37; Posy Simmonds 18; Tony Stone World Wide *cover*; Topham 6, 14, 19, 20, 23, 31, 40; Wayland Picture Library 25 (Chris Schwarz), 30, 34; Timothy Woodcock 33; Zefa Picture Library 28, 44. The artworks on pages 11 and 38 were supplied by Malcolm S Walker.

Index

Page numbers in bold refer to illustrations

LEABHARLANN
CHONDAE AN CHABHAIN

1. This book may be kept three weeks.
   It is to be returned on / before the last date
   stamped below.
2. A fine of 20p will be charged for every week
   or part of week a book is overdue.
